Second Memento Workshop on Modelling Parameters of Cognitive Effort in Translation Production 2019

Held at Machine Translation Summit XVII

Dublin, Ireland
20 August 2019

ISBN: 978-1-5108-9248-4

Printed from e-media with permission by:

Curran Associates, Inc.
57 Morehouse Lane
Red Hook, NY 12571

Some format issues inherent in the e-media version may also appear in this print version.

Printed by Curran Associates, Inc. (2019)

For permission requests, please contact the Association for Computational Linguistics at the address below.

Association for Computational Linguistics
209 N. Eighth Street
Stroudsburg, Pennsylvania 18360

Phone: 1-570-476-8006
Fax: 1-570-476-0860

acl@aclweb.org

Additional copies of this publication are available from:

Curran Associates, Inc.
57 Morehouse Lane
Red Hook, NY 12571 USA
Phone: 845-758-0400
Fax: 845-758-2633
Email: curran@proceedings.com
Web: www.proceedings.com

Machine Translation Summit XVII

DUBLIN
MACHINE
TRANSLATION
SUMMIT 2019

Second MEMENTO workshop on Modelling Parameters of Cognitive Effort in Translation Production

20 August, 2019
Dublin, Ireland

Second MEMENTO workshop on Modelling Parameters of Cognitive Effort in Translation Production

20 August, 2019
Dublin, Ireland

Preface from the co-chairs of the workshop

Over the last three decades empirical Translation Process Research (TPR) has been prolific in the generation of hypothesis and models, which were based mostly on insights drawn from from-scratch translation. More recently, TPR has also addressed - among other things - post-editing and spoken translation (sight translation, interpretation), and tried to come up with more comprehensive cognitive models of the translation process which are based on empirical data and include various dichotomies, such as comprehension/production, speaking/writing, manual/computer assisted translation, etc. In order to address those newly emerging research questions, the MEMENTO project boosts empirical TPR by organizing yearly international 'bootcamps' to elaborate and investigate TPR-related research hypotheses over a three to four-week period and by disseminating the results of those bootcamps in successive conferences and workshops. The first MEMENTO bootcamp took place in July 2018 at the University of Macau, and a successive first MEMENTO workshop was conducted in November 2018 in Beijing in the context of the 5th International Conference on Cognitive Research on Translation and Interpreting. The second MEMENTO bootcamp took place in July / August 2019 at Kent State University/USA. Approximately 20 early and more matured researchers discussed, developed, and proto-typed methods and solutions to address and evaluate TPR-related hypothesis over a four-week period. The Second MEMENTO workshop – conducted in the context of the MT-Summit 2019 in Dublin - is a forum to present and discuss some of the outcomes of this four-weeks bootcamp in a public space, and to gather feedback and input for the continuation of the MEMENTO project(s) in the future. It therefore contains several contributions from participants of the first and the second MEMENTO bootcamp, but also a small number of abstracts from presenters who did not attend the MEMENTO bootcamps (yet). We collected 12 abstracts covering a range of TPR-related topics, including aspects of cognitive load in written and spoken translation, addressing issues in translation difficulty and translation quality assessment, translations of metaphors and neologisms, as well as audio-visual translation and lexical representation. We hope to have compiled a collection of abstracts that covers many of the topics for Modelling Parameters of Cognitive Effort in Translation Production.

We look forward to welcoming you at the Second MEMENTO workshop 2019 in Dublin.

Michael Carl and Silvia Hansen-Schirra

Organizers

Workshop Chairs

Michael Carl
Silvia Hansen-Schirra

Program Committee

Aljoscha Burchardt,
Binghan Zheng,
David Orrego-Carmona,
Defeng Li,
Fabio Alves,
Haidee Kruger,
Irina Temnikova,
Isabel Lacruz,
Joke Daems,
Lucas Vieira,
Masaru Yamada,
Moritz Schaeffer,
Sharon O'Brien,
Victoria Lei

Contents

Edit distances do not describe editing, but they can be useful for translation process research

Félix do Carmo
ADAPT Centre / Dublin City University
CTTS - Centre for Translation and Textual Studies / Dublin City University
felix.docarmo@adaptcentre.ie

Abstract

Translation process research (TPR) aims at describing what translators do, and one of the technical dimensions of translators' work is editing (applying detailed changes to text). In this presentation, we will analyze how different methods for process data collection describe editing. We will review keyloggers used in typical TPR applications, track changes used by word processors, and edit rates based on estimation of edit distances. The purpose of this presentation is to discuss the limitations of these methods when describing editing behavior, and to incentivize researchers in looking for ways to present process data in simplified formats, closer to those that describe product data.

1 Research background

The technical dimension of translation, revision and post-editing is characterized by writing actions. Editing, part of this technical dimension, is a set of actions that is applied to pre-existing text. This implies that editing cannot be analyzed in the same way as translating or writing from scratch. We see editing as being composed of four actions: delete, insert, move and replace (do Carmo 2017). This presentation discusses the implications of this definition of editing and of different methods to describe it.

If we want to know which words were edited and how, we need data that accurately describes the actions performed. After we have that data, we may extract from it features that can be used to train computational models that predict editing patterns and behaviors.

TPR tools, like Translog II (Carl, 2012) and Inputlog (Leijten and Van Waes, 2013) use keylogging to collect process data, in a character and chronological base. However, it has been shown that it is not straightforward to convert TPR data into word-based sequences of edit actions (do Carmo et al., 2018; Leijten et al., 2012). The main reason for this is the fact that process data is not linear: it includes incomplete, repeated, wrong actions, scattered edits, and other process components that cannot be associated with the words that survive in the final edited versions.

Word processors and translation tools often incorporate track change features that record editing, but these too are not straightforwardly converted into editing data.

Product data seems to describe a simpler reality, so simpler methods may be used. Edit distances appeared in the 1960's as methods to identify and correct errors of spelling in text typing (Damerau, 1964), and errors in computer code (Levenshtein, 1966). These edit distances evolved into metrics like WER–Word Error Rate (Popovic and Ney, 2007) and TER–Translation Edit Rate (Snover et al., 2006), both of which have several variants.

Edit rates identify differences between two versions of a text, and they have been extensively used in applications like automatic post-editing (do Carmo et al, 2019) and quality estimation of machine translation (Specia et al., 2018). In these applications, they are seen as good predictors of the editing required by texts or sentences.

2 Experiment

We conducted a brief experiment to assess the capacity of different methods to identify the editing actions actually performed by translators. We created a test set of a few sentences to which we simulated the application of edits in a sequence of growing complexity. This experiment allowed us to describe the structure of different data collection and analysis methods and to show their limitations in identifying the actions that were performed on one version of a text to transform it into another version. Methods like TER are analysed and described in detail.

3 Results and discussion

One of the conclusions of the experiment above is that edit distances should not be used as descriptors of processes. Nevertheless, edit distances are very useful. Their power lies in their intuitiveness and descriptive capacity: everything is a change in a unit, in a position, or in both. And four actions only (delete, insert, replace and move) describe all transformations that can be done to a sentence. But the main contribution of these metrics is the efficiency requirement – the aim is to identify the 'minimum distance' from one string to the other. This has led to an oversimplified view of editing, but it may have a positive use.

For the TPR community, it would be useful to have a description of editing work that benefited from these simplified descriptions. There would be obvious advantages in converting process data into formats inspired by editing rates. One of the advantages would be that machine translation researchers could more easily integrate the knowledge created by the TPR community. Besides, based on simpler data descriptions, more complex research can be done, enabling us to test further dimensions of editing, like the relation between edit rates and technical effort, or to study different rates of intensity of editing in translation, revision and post-editing.

Acknowledgements

This Project has received funding from the European Union's Horizon 2020 research and innovation programme under the EDGE COFUND Marie Skłodowska-Curie Grant Agreement no. 713567. This publication has emanated from research supported in part by a research grant from Science Foundation Ireland (SFI) under Grant Number 13/RC/2077.

References

Carl, Michael. 2012. Translog-II: a Program for Recording User Activity Data for Empirical Translation Process Research. *LREC 2012, 8th International Conference on Language Resources and Evaluation.* Istanbul (Vol. 3, pp. 153–162).

Damerau, Fred J. 1964. A Technique for Computer Detection and Correction of Spelling Errors. *Communications of the ACM* 7 (3): 171–76. https://doi.org/10.1145/363958.363994.

do Carmo, Félix. 2017. "Post-Editing: A Theoretical and Practical Challenge for Translation Studies and Machine Learning." Universidade do Porto. https://repositorio-aberto.up.pt/handle/10216/107518.

do Carmo, Félix, Klaus Buchegger, Rossana Cunha, and Michael Carl. 2018. New Ways of Describing Editing in TPR-DB. *5th International Conference on Cognitive Research on Translation and Interpreting.* Beijing, China.

do Carmo, Félix. et al. 2019. 'A Review of the State-of-the-art in Automatic Post-editing', *Machine Translation*, (forthcoming).

Leijten, Mariëlle, & Luuk van Waes. 2013. Keystroke Logging in Writing Research: Using Inputlog to Analyze and Visualize Writing Processes. *Written Communication* 30(3), 358–392 doi: 10.1177/0741088313491692

Leijten, Mariëlle, et al. 2012. From Character to Word Level: Enabling the Linguistic Analyses of Inputlog Process Data. *EACL-Computational Linguistics and Writing (CL&W 2012): Linguistic and Cognitive Aspects of Document Creation and Document Engineering*, 1–8.

Levenshtein, Vladimir I. 1966. Binary Codes Capable of Correcting Deletions, Insertions and Reversals. *Soviet Physics Doklady* 10 (8): 707–710.

Popovič, Maja, Hermann Ney. 2007. Word error rates: decomposition over POS classes and applications for error analysis. *Proceedings of the 2nd workshop on Statistical Machine Translation (WMT 2007),* Prague, pp 48–55

Snover, Matthew, Bonnie Dorr, Richard Schwartz, Linnea Micciulla, and John Makhoul. 2006. A Study of Translation Edit Rate with Targeted Human Annotation. *Proceedings of AMTA 2006,* August: 223–31. https://doi.org/10.1.1.129.4369.

Specia, Lúcia, Scarton, Carolina and Paetzold, Gustavo. 2018. *Quality estimation for machine translation.* Morgan & Claypool. doi: 10.2200/S00854ED1V01Y201805HLT039.

Modelling word translation entropy and syntactic equivalence with machine learning

Bram Vanroy, Orphée De Clercq, Lieve Macken
LT[3], Language and Translation Technology Team
Ghent University
Belgium
firstname.lastname@ugent.be

Previous research suggests that translation product features such as word translation entropy (WTE) and the degree of syntactic equivalence (SE) correlate with cognitive load (Schaeffer et al. (2016)), and Sun (2015), respectively). WTE quantifies the number of translation choices at word level that a translator is confronted with, whereas SE quantifies the syntactic (dis)similarity between a source and target text. In Vanroy et al. (2019), we found that when a source word has multiple possible translations (WTE), a translator may require more cognitive effort to find the suitable translation; and different syntactic structures of the source segment vis-à-vis the proposed target segment may lead to an increased cognitive effort (SE). Consequently, a high average WTE or dissimilar syntactic structures for a given source text and its translation would indicate that a text was difficult to translate.

The current research aims to predict WTE of a source text as well as its SE to a target text without having access to the actual translation products. We do that by training machine learning (ML) systems on a parallel corpus to model these features. We focus on English to Dutch translation, and we use the Dutch Parallel Corpus (Macken et al. (2011); DPC) as our parallel dataset. Unlike the work done in the Translation Process Research Database (Carl et al., 2016) which uses multiple translations of the same text, we calculate a word's translation entropy based on how it has been translated across the whole corpus. We investigate different ML architectures, and features ranging from the sentence to the morphosyntactic level (for the latter, see Tezcan et al. (2017)). The goal is that by only feeding a source sentence into the systems, they can predict that sentence's average WTE and SE.

In addition, we investigate whether we can go one step further and use machine translation (MT) systems as an approximation for human translations for the specific task above. This would mean that we do not need human translations nor ML, and that we can confidently use MT to generate a translation and calculate WTE and SE between the source text and the machine translated target text. To explore the feasibility of this approach, we reuse WTE and SE that were calculated on DPC. Then we translate the source text of that corpus with MT and calculate WTE and SE for these translations. Correlating the WTE and SE values from the human translations and those of the MT version indicates how confidently MT can be used as a proxy for human translations in this task.

This study is carried out in the framework of the PreDicT project[1] (Predicting Difficulty in Translation), which aims to develop a translatability prediction system for English-Dutch that not only automatically assigns a global difficulty score to a given source text, but also identifies the passages in the source text that are difficult to translate.

References

Carl, M., Schaeffer, M. J., and Bangalore, S. (2016). The CRITT translation process research database. In Carl, M., Bangalore, S., and Schaeffer, M. J., editors, *New directions in empirical translation process research*, New frontiers in translation studies, pages 13–54. Springer, Cham, Switzerland.

[1] https://research.flw.ugent.be/en/projects/predict

Macken, L., De Clercq, O., and Paulussen, H. (2011). Dutch parallel corpus: A balanced copyright-cleared parallel corpus. *Meta: Journal des traducteurs*, 56(2):374–390.

Schaeffer, M., Dragsted, B., Hvelplund, K. T., Balling, L. W., and Carl, M. (2016). Word translation entropy: Evidence of early target language activation during reading for translation. In Carl, M., Bangalore, S., and Schaeffer, M., editors, *New directions in empirical translation process research*, pages 183–210. Springer International Publishing, Cham, Switzerland.

Sun, S. (2015). Measuring translation difficulty: Theoretical and methodological considerations. *Across languages and cultures*, 16(1):29–54.

Tezcan, A., Hoste, V., and Macken, L. (2017). A neural network architecture for detecting grammatical errors in statistical machine translation. *The Prague bulletin of mathematical linguistics*, 108(1):133–145.

Vanroy, B., De Clercq, O., and Macken, L. (2019). Correlating process and product data to get an insight into translation difficulty. *Perspectives*, pages 1–18.

Comparison of temporal, technical and cognitive dimension measurements for post-editing effort

Cristina Cumbreño and Nora Aranberri
IXA research group
University of the Basque Country UPV/EHU
{ccumbreno001,nora.aranberri}@ehu.eus

Abstract

This work aims to take a step towards understanding the relationship between the different dimensions of the post-editing effort. Specifically, we perform a preliminary experiment where temporal, technical and cognitive effort measurements are collected for six error types using mainstream tools. Results seem to indicate that when considered in isolation, errors do not pose significant differences in effort within each dimension. We also find that measurements of different tools do not always correlate.

1 Introduction

Post-editing remuneration sits somewhere between translation and proofreading rates motivated by the assumption that post-editing is faster than translating from scratch but machine translation quality does not consistently allow for swift proofreading. Whereas pricing should be a compromise for both companies and translators, it is still common to hear of frustrated translators complaining about post-editing rates. These tend to be established following productivity tests which mainly consider time differences between translation from scratch and post-editing. There is still no conclusive evidence, however, that this measure captures the full effort involved in post-editing.

According to Krings (2001), there are three dimensions to post-editing effort: temporal, technical and cognitive. Also, some research suggests that different errors require varying effort (Koponen, 2012; Lacruz, Denkowski and Lavie, 2014; Popovic et al., 2014; Daems et al., 2015). In this preliminary work, we aim to analyse the performance of different commonly used measurements when addressing concrete error types. Specifically, we focus on time, keystroke and reported perception information to investigate (1) whether these measurements detect differences in error types and (2) to what extent they agree on the measured post-editing effort.

2 Experimental Set-up

Following the advice of different authors (Burchardt et al., 2016; Guillou and Hardmeier, 2016; Schaeffer et al., 2019), we opted for a test suite to control as many external factors as possible and isolate specific errors within the sentences. We studied six error types, which belong to different categories of the cognitive difficulty classification by Temnikova (2010), namely, agreements (number/gender and verbal aspect/mode), mistranslations (one word and multiple words), and extra and missing words. The final test suite consisted of 10 sentences per error. The 60 sentences were automatically translated from the original English source language to Spanish using Google Translator and post-edited by 7 professional translators. Even when we are aware that this approach might reduce the ecological validity of the results, it is the most accurate way to collect the specific effort brought by each error, which is essential at this preliminary stage of the research.

Participants worked on a PET (Aziz et al., 2012) project, where we were able to collect information that is assumed to reflect temporal, technical and cognitive effort. Specifically, we collected total time, total pause time, total pause count, length of initial pause, length of final pause, length of pauses during editing and number of pauses during editing as measures for the temporal dimension; keystrokes and HTER for the technical dimension and perceived reported effort for the cognitive dimension.

3 Results and Conclusions

Preliminary results show that raw time counts seem to be similar for all error types whereas certain differences, albeit minimal, are revealed when considering keystrokes and perceived effort. Post-editing missing words and mistranslations results in a higher number of keystrokes and higher perceived difficulty. Overall, we also observe that the correlations between the measurements of time, keystrokes and perceived effort are lower than 0.4, which seems to indicate that using the results for the dimensions separately does not reveal the full effort involved in post-editing.

Acknowledgements: The research leading to this work was partially funded by the Modena project of the Department of Economic Development and Infrastructures of the Basque Government (KK-2018/00087), the UnsupNMT project (TIN201791692EXP - MEC), and the Domino project (PGC2018-102041-B-I00 - MCIU/AEI/FEDER, UE).

References

Aziz, Wiker, Sheila C. M. Sousa and Lucia Specia. 2012. PET: A Tool for Post-editing and Assessing Machine Translation. *Proceedings of the 8th International Conference on Language Resources and Evaluation*, Istanbul, Turkey. 3982–3987.

Burchardt, Aljoscha, Kim Harris, Georg Rehm, and Hans Uszkoreit 2016. Towards a Systematic and Human-Informed Paradigm for High-Quality Machine Translation. *Proceedings of the LREC 2016 Workshop Translation Evaluation From Fragmented Tools and Data Sets to an Integrated Ecosystem*, Portoro, Slovenia. 35–42.

Daems, Joke, Sonia Vandepitte, Robert Hartsuiker and Lieve Macken. 2015. The impact of machine translation error types on post-editing effort indicators. *Proceedings of the Fourth Workshop on Post-Editing Technology and Practice*, Miami, Florida. 31–45.

Guillou, Liane and Christian Hardmeier 2016. PROTEST: A Test Suit for Evaluating Pronouns in Machine Translation. *Proceedings of the Tenth International Conference on Language Resources and Evaluation*, Portoro, Slovenia. 636–643.

Koponen, Maarit. 2012. Comparing human perceptionsof post-editing effort with post-editing operations. *Proceedings of the 7th Workshop on Statistical Machine Translation*, Montral, Canada. 181–190.

Krings, Hans P. 2001. *Repairing texts: empirical investigations of machine translation post-editing processes.* Kent State University Press, Kent, Ohio and London.

Lacruz, Isabel, Michael Denkowski and Alon Lavie. 2014. Cognitive Demand and Cognitive Effort in Post-Editing. *Proceedings of the Third Workshop on Post-Editing Technology and Practice*, Vancouver, Canada. 73–84.

Popovic, Maja, Arle Lommel, Aljoscha Burchardt, Eleftherios Avramidis, and Hans Uszkoreit. 2014. Relations between different types of post-editing operations, cognitive effort and temporal effort. *Proceedings of the 17th Annual Conference of the European Association for Machine Translation*, Dubrovnik, Croatia. 191–45.

Schaeffer, Moritz, Jean Nitzke, Anke Tardel, Katharina Oster, Silke Gutermuth and Silvia Hansen-Schirra. 2019. Eye-tracking revision processes of translation students and professional translators. *Perspectives, 27:4*. 589–603.

Temnikova, Irina. 2010. Cognitive Evaluation Approach for a Controlled Language Post-Editing Experiment. *Proceedings of the seventh international conference on Language Resources and Evaluation*, Valletta, Malta. 3485–3490.

Translation Quality and Effort Prediction in Professional Machine Translation Post-Editing

Jennifer Vardaro
Johannes Gutenberg University
Mainz, Germany
vardaro@uni-mainz.de

Moritz Schaeffer
Johannes Gutenberg University
Mainz, Germany
mschae01@uni-mainz.de

Silvia Hansen-Schirra
Johannes Gutenberg University
Mainz, Germany
hansenss@uni-mainz.de

Abstract

The focus of this controlled eye-tracking and key-logging study is to analyze the behaviour of translation professionals at the European Commission's Directorate-General for Translation (DGT) when detecting and correcting errors in neural machine translated texts (NMT) and their post-edited versions (NMTPE). The experiment was informed by quality analyses of an authentic DGT parallel corpus (Vardaro, Schaeffer, and Hansen-Schirra 2019), consisting of English source texts and corresponding German NMT, NMTPE and revisions (REV). To identify the most characteristic error categories in NMT and NMTPE, we used the automatic error annotation tool Hjerson (Popović 2011) and the more fine-grained manual MQM framework (Lommel 2014). Results show that quality assurance measures by post-editors and revisors at the DGT are most often necessary for lexical errors. More specifically, if post-editors correct mistranslations, terminology or stylistic errors in an NMT sentence, revisors are likely to correct the same type of error in the same sentence, suggesting a certain transitivity between the NMT system and human post-editors.

In this study, carried out in Translog II (Carl 2012), participants' eye movements and typing behavior for test sentences where the error categories mistranslation, terminology, function words and stylistic errors are included will be compared to control sentences without errors. 30 language professionals from the DGT post-edited 100 English-German machine translated sentences from the DGT corpus. We examine the three error types' effect on early (first fixation durations, first pass durations) and late eye movement measures (e.g., total reading time and regression path duration) and on typing behaviour. Statistical regression analyses predict the temporal, technical, and cognitive effort during the DGT post-editing and revision process which will be corelated to the recognition and correction of said error categories. In addition, the behavioural data of the DGT translation professionals will be compared to those of a group of 30 translation students. Behavioural differences in the two groups will allow for further predictions regarding the effect of expertise on the post-editing process.in

References

Carl, Michael. 2012. 'Translog-II: A Program for Recording User Activity Data for Empirical Translation Process Research'. *International Journal of Computational Linguistics and Applications*, 2012.

Lommel, Arle. 2014. 'Multidimensional Quality Metrics Definition'. 2014. http://www.qt21.eu/mqm-definition/definition-2015-06-16.html.

Popović, Maja. 2011. 'Hjerson: An Open Source Tool for Automatic Error Classification of Machine Translation Output'. *The Prague Bulletin of Mathematical Linguistics* 96 (1). https://doi.org/10.2478/v10108-011-0011-4.

Vardaro, Jennifer, Moritz Schaeffer, and Silvia Hansen-Schirra. 2019. 'Comparing the Quality of Neural Machine Translation and Professional Post-Editing'. In *Proceedings of QoMEX*, 1–3. Berlin, Germany. https://doi.org/10.1109/QoMEX.2019.8743218.

With or without post-editing processes? Evidence for a gap in machine translation evaluation

Caroline Rossi
Univ. Grenoble Alpes (ICEA4)
France
Caroline.Rossi@univ-grenoble-alpes.fr

Emmanuelle Esperança-Rodier
Univ. Grenoble Alpes (LIG)
France
Emmanuelle.Esperanca-Rodier@univ-grenoble-alpes.fr

Abstract

Machine translation evaluation (MTE) is performed differently and with different goals in academia and industry (Drugan 2013, in Castilho et al. 2018 : 11). However, with the current integration of neural machine translation into human translation workflows, reliable measures of the amount of effort needed to post-edit machine translation (PEMT) outputs have become a common goal for researchers, language service providers and machine translation vendors (ibid., p. 29). Translation process research has developed tools to gather and analyse empirical data, but while a variety of measures have proved useful and reliable to measure PEMT effort (see e.g. Vieira 2016 : 42), translation processes are seldom considered when assessing the relevance of a given MTPE scenario.

Against this background, our study seeks to determine the impact of including MTPE in the evaluation process. We selected two of the most commonly used scales for the "declarative evaluation" of MT (Humphreys et al. 1991, in Way 2018b : 164): adequacy and fluency ratings. Based on two distinct experimental conditions, we then compared the ratings produced without performing PE and those produced immediately after a light PE process.

Data was collected with a group of 14 trainee translators, using two different text types and two different tools. A first series of assessments was conducted with KantanMT's language quality review system (LQR), which allows for a simple comparative evaluation of two systems without post-editing the outputs. The second series was done a few weeks later, in Post-Editing Tool (PET, Aziz et al. 2012). Each experimental condition includes two source texts from two different domains (environmental discourse and patents). We generated usable SMT and NMT outputs using eTranslation with environmental texts and WIPO translate with patent extracts. In both conditions, the students were given a realistic scenario -- i.e. they performed the evaluation, with a view to determining whether the MT output was relevant to a particular order.

Interrater reliability was assessed for each segment in each text (N=55) using Fleiss' kappa for adequacy and fluency scores, and an intraclass correlation coefficient (Vieira 2016 : 52) for temporal measures. While the reliability of the measures collected without PE was low, the measures collected in PET were for the most part homogeneous. Thus, evaluation was more reliable when performed with PE than without. Similarly, and even though there was more variation in temporal measures, homogeneity was stronger in PET data, suggesting that the activity was performed in a similar way across trainee translators.

We finally sought to determine what went wrong by performing qualitative analyses of the problematic segments, as evidenced by both kappa and intraclass correlation coefficients. Overall, our results suggest that it is very difficult, at least for trainee translators, to assess MT without PE. Specific training combining MTPE and evaluation might be particularly helpful to prepare them for a changing industry.

References

Aziz W, Sousa SCM, Specia L (2012). PET: a tool for post-editing and assessing machine translation. In: Calzolari N, Choukri K, Declerck T, Dogan MU, Maegaard B, Mariani J, Moreno A, Odijk J, Piperidis S (eds) *Proceedings of the eighth international conference on language resources and evaluation*, Istanbul, pp 3982–3987.

Castilho, S., Doherty, S., Gaspari, F., & Moorkens, J. (2018). Approaches to human and machine translation quality assessment. In *Translation Quality Assessment* (pp. 9-38). Springer, Cham.

Vieira, L. N. (2016). How do measures of cognitive effort relate to each other? A multivariate analysis of post-editing process data. *Machine Translation, 30*(1-2), 41-62.

Way A (2018a) Machine translation: where are we at today? In: Angelone E, Massey G, Ehrensberger-Dow M (eds) *The Bloomsbury companion to language industry studies*. Bloomsbury, London.

Way, A. (2018b) Quality expectations of machine translation. In *Translation Quality Assessment* (pp. 159-178). Springer, Cham.

Investigating Correlations Between Human Translation and MT Output

Samar A. Almazroei
Kent State University
475 Janik Drive, Kent, OH
44242 | Satterfield H. 109
salmazr1@kent.edu

Haruka Ogawa
Kent State University
475 Janik Drive, Kent, OH
44242 | Satterfield H. 109
hogawa@kent.edu

Devin Gilbert
Kent State University
475 Janik Drive, Kent, OH
44242 | Satterfield H. 109
dgilbe10@kent.edu

Abstract

This study investigates whether there is a correlation between machine translation (MT) and human translation (HT) in terms of word translation entropy (i.e., the variance observed in different translations based on the same source text). Our analysis showed a significant strong correlation in all the three languages we examined: Arabic, Japanese, and Spanish. Furthermore, MT, as well as HT, was found to correlate across languages, although the associations were weaker than the MT-HT correlation in each language.

1 Introduction

This study explores the relationship between the variance in translation output from multiple MT systems and multiple alternative human translations of the same source texts (ST) in three different languages: Arabic, Japanese, and Spanish. Previous studies have reported a correlation between the number of translation options in MT and HT for the same ST words, which leads to the assumption that both MT engines and humans face similar decision-making difficulties within the same language and across different languages (e.g., Carl & Schaeffer 2017, Carl & Báez 2019).

In order to test this hypothesis, the current study first investigates whether the word translation entropy (designated as HTra; see Carl et al. (2016)) of MT output correlates with that of HT in each language. We further investigate to what extent word translation entropy for MT and HT correlates across the three languages. We then conduct qualitative analyses to explore the commonalities and differences among the three languages by comparing the cases where HTra values are high in both MT and HT.

2 Procedure

We used the multiLing texts of the Translation Process Research Database (TPR-DB), which consists of six texts comprising a total of ST 847 tokens and 40 segments. Each text was translated using commercially available MT systems: 12 different systems for Arabic, 13 for Japanese, and 9 for Spanish (for a full list of these systems, see Appendix A).

After obtaining the MT output, the target tokens in each language were aligned componentially to their corresponding English source tokens using Yawat (Germann, 2008). Tokens were aligned on a semantic basis while trying to break phrases down to the smallest units possible, with consistency being key in order for the HTra metric to only reflect output variance and not differences in alignment. For example, if an MT system translates the news story headline "Killer Nurse receives four life sentences" as "*La enfermera del asesino recibe cuatro condenas a cadena perpetua*," 'Killer' would be aligned with '*del asesino*,' 'Nurse' with '*La enfermera*,' 'receives' with '*recibe*,' 'four,' with '*cuatro*,' 'sentences' with '*condenas*,' and 'life' with '*a cadena perpetua*.' The data was then transformed into tables according to TPR-DB conventions. The metric we use in this study (i.e., HTra values) was also calculated according to the same conventions.

3 Results

As shown in Figure 1, results of the Spearman correlation indicated that there is a strong and significant positive association between the HTra of Japanese MT output (HTraJAMT) and that of Japanese HT output (HTraENJA) ($r(845) = .66$, $p < .001$), between Spanish MT output (HTraESMT) and Spanish HT (HTraBML) ($r(845)=.61$, $p<.001$), as well as Arabic MT (HTraARMT) and Arabic HT (HTraAR19) ($r(845)=.62$, $p<.001$). Across the three languages, weak positive correlations were found for MT, and moderate positive correlations for HT (see Figure 1).

Within these instances, there were only 16 cases where the HTra values were ranked in the top 20 in all the languages. The words "hunter" and "gatherer" in "hunter-gatherer societies" accounted for 6 of these instances. The other instances were mostly idiomatic expressions (i.e., "the extra green mile" and "flaring up") and/or figurative use of verbs (i.e., *hit* as in "Families hit with increase in cost of living" and *flaring up* as in "His withdrawal comes in the wake of fighting flaring up again").

Although all three languages had verb-type tags as the most frequently occurring PoS in their top 20 HTra values, the highest HTra values in the Arabic and Japanese datasets correspond to the 'TO' and 'DT' (determiner) tags, respectively (tags are from the Penn Treebank Project). In the Spanish dataset, however, verb-type tags were the highest and most frequent PoS tags.

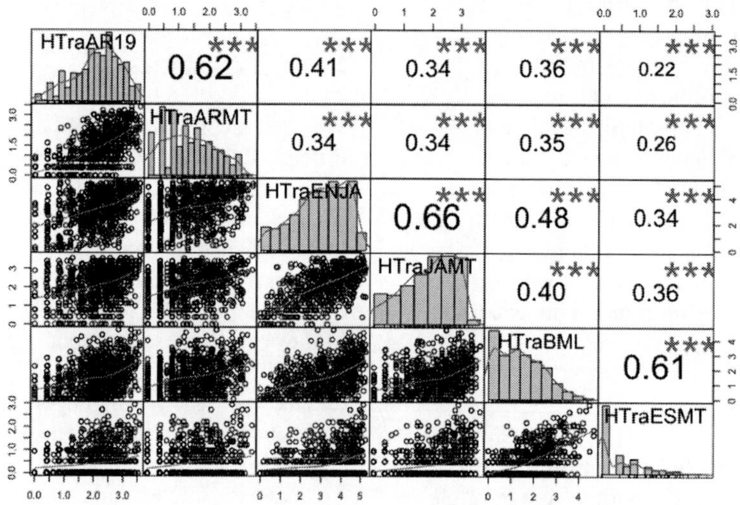

Figure 1: Correlation within and across the three languages

4 Discussion

The correlation between MT and HT was the strongest in Japanese, followed by Arabic and then Spanish. The correlation across languages was moderate for the combination of Arabic and Japanese, and Japanese and Spanish, and weak between Arabic and Spanish. Although the correlations found across languages were weaker than those found within each language, all correlations were still significant (see figure 1).

For qualitative analyses, we ranked the HTra values in each study and examined, for each text in each language, the top 20 tokens and their part of speech (PoS). 51 instances in Arabic and Japanese respectively and 66 in Spanish were found where the HTra values were ranked in the top 20 for both MT and HT.

5 Remarks

This study reveals intriguing results on the relationship between MT and HT. Further investigations will be conducted to explore whether MT output can be considered as a reliable predictor for human translation effort. In the future, we would like to expand the language variation and examine the commonalities and differences across different languages more qualitatively.

References

Carl, Michael; Schaeffer, Moritz; & Bangalore, Srinivas (2016). The CRITT translation process research database. In *New directions in empirical translation process research* (pp. 13–54). Springer.

Carl, M., & Schaeffer, M. J. (2017). Why translation is difficult: A corpus-based study of non-literality in post-editing and from-scratch translation. HERMES-Journal of Language and Communication in Business, (56), 43-57.

Carl, M., & Báez, M. C. T. (2019). Machine translation errors and the translation process: a study across different languages. Journal of Specialised Translation, (31), 107-132.

Germann, Ulrich (2008). Yawat: yet another word alignment tool. *Proceedings of the 46th Annual Meeting of the Association for Computational Linguistics on Human Language Technologies: Demo Session*, 20–23. Association for Computational Linguistics.

Appendix A. MT Systems Used

Arabic: Amazon Translate, Bing, DayTranslations, Google, Online English Arabic Translator, Prompt Online, Reverso, Systran, Tradukka, Translator.eu, Translatr, and Yandex.

Japanese: Baidu, Bing, Excite, Google, Paralink ImTranslator, Infoseek, MiraiTranslate, Pragma, So-Net, Textra, Weblio, WorldLingo, and Yandex.

Spanish: Amazon Translate, Baidu, Bing, DeepL, Google, Lilt, Pragma, Yarakuzen, and Yandex.

Lexical Representation & Retrieval on Monolingual Interpretative text production

Debasish Sahoo
Kent State University, USA
dsahoo@kent.edu

Dr. Michael Carl
Kent State University, USA
mcarl6@kent.edu

Abstract

Over the past decade, researches in the domain of Language Translation have grown multi-folds. One such area of focus is how the words are encoded, stored and retrieved from memory of individuals who are involved in process of text translation and production. Several models have been developed around this research area, among which Bilingual Interaction Activation (BIA and BIA+) and Multilink are two such popular models with precise hypothesis which can be tested. In this paper, we shall primarily focus to investigate, how the above models assumptions on lexical access (how the words are activated and retrieved in human memory during text production tasks) impact the text production time. Though the above models are designed for bilingual translations, they can also be applied to monolingual tasks. We will limit our experiment to monolingual interpretative text production tasks : Copying, Paraphrasing and Summarizing, in English language only.

1 Introduction

BIA model, in its original form emphasised only on the orthographic representation of the words and its framework was based on a monolingual Interactive Activation Model (IAM). It assumes that during lexical access, words similar in orthography get activated in the mind of the of the user. In case of Bilingual Translation, both the languages are active in the user's memory. Subsequent versions of BIA model (BIA+), took into account the role of phonology (similar sounding) and semantics (similar meaning) during lexical access. Multilink, in addition, assumes that the already activated orthographic neighbors based on the input word activate their associated semantic neighbors, which in turn activate their associated phonetic neighbours and so on. The model explains the observed increase in the word production time by the co-existance of the so many similar words in user's mind. In this paper, we will assess the Multilink hypothesis on the monolingual interpretative text production task. Copying amounts to the most conceivable literal interpretation of a text and thus constitutes a baseline for interpretative text production. Translation can be considered interpretative text production (Gutt, 2010), but other types of monolingual interpretative text production include paraphrasing and summarizing. We operationalize orthographic and semantic similarity by using the measures Orthographic Neighbours (ONS) and Semantic Neighbours (SNS) respectively. Our hypothesis is that the the presence of larger set of such similar words is directly proportional to the word production time.

2 Experiment

For our experiment, we used the *Multiling* dataset from *CriTT TPR-DB* consisting of 6 different English texts. 13 students from the Computer Science department, all proficient in the English language were assigned to perform 3 different tasks - *Copying(C), Paraphrasing(H) and Summarizing(U)*. 9 of these students were native English speakers and 4 of them were Indian students. These tasks were performed on our laboratory computer configured with *EyeTracker (SMI 250mobile) and Keystroke Logger (Translog-II)*. The data was then uploaded to *Translation Process Research (TPR)* database and aligned. We used Python based libraries (Pandas, Numpy and Matplotlib) on Jupyter Notebooks to execute our experiment.

3 Data

Below are some of the important behavioral data captured in the TPR-DB

SToken represents the source text word token

TGroup represents produced word(s) corresponding to its SToken

Dur provides the word-production time (in ms) for each SToken

HTra provides the Translational Cross Entropy for each SToken

Ins, Del provides the Num of Insertions and Deletions to produce each TGroup for its SToken

4 Orthographic Similarity

According to BIA, *Orthographic Neighbours* are defined by words that differ only by 1 letter. These words look similar to the eyes of the user. According to the BIA, while performing any word production task, the orthographically similar words corresponding to the word being processed, get activated in the user's mind which leads to delay and subsequent longer word production time. In our experiment, we use *Levenshtein Distance (LD)* to find the *Orthographic Neighbours* of our SToken and refer the term Orthographic Neighbours Set (ONS) for the list of such words. The *LD* is a string metric for measuring the difference between two sequences. Informally, the LD between two words is the minimum number of single-character edits (insertions, deletions or substitutions) required to change one word into the other. *ONS* for a SToken is defined as the set of all the words with LD = 1 found in the word-token repository(BNC). For example, ONS for *"killing"*, is {*"willing","filling","billing","milling","tilling" ,"pilling","killings", "skilling"*}.

We used the *British National Corpus (BNC)* as the reference corpus to create word-token repository. The pre-processing steps include tokenizing the corpus to word-tokens, cleaning to remove alpha-nums, numeric, tokens with special characters, grouping the unique word-tokens by its frequency of occurrence in the corpus. Lastly, the tokens are stored as key,value pairs with each word as key and its frequency as value after removing the words with frequency < 10, since they might be typos. We have around 600,000 unique tokens in the repository.

After computing the ONS for all STokens, we used the below measure (SimS1) to calculate the orthographic similarity score for our hypothesis

$$SimS1 = \sum_{s \in ONS} 1 - (lev/len(s))$$

where s = size of ONS, lev = LD and len(s) = length of the word in ONS.

We observe a negative effect (p-value of 0.46) of the ONS on the Word Production Duration. The higher p-value suggests that our results are not significant. These results are not in accordance to the hypothesis laid down in BIA. Hence, we can accept our Null Hypothesis

5 Semantic Similarity

The semantic neighbours of a word is defined as the list of words with similar meaning. We generate the Semantic Neighbours Set (SNS) consisting of semantically similar words using the Word2Vec.

Word2Vec (Word2Vec, 2008a) is a popular word-embedding model, which once trained, can be used to find semantically similar words given an input word. We used a python based framework Gensim and a pre-trained word-embedding model provided by *(Global Vectors for Word Representation)* (glove.6B.100d.zip) to load our Word2Vec model. The Glove model are trained on a corpus containing 6 Billion word tokens, with each word vector represented in 100 dimensions. This model uses cosine similarity to find list of similar words along with its similarity score (SS) - between 0 and 1. We only include words with SS $>$ 0.7 for our test. SNS for a SToken is defined as the set of all the words with SS $>$ 0.7. For e.g. ONS for *"killing"* is {*"murders","slaying","shooting","kidnappings", "executions", "deaths","arrests",*} .

We used the measure *SemanticSim* (the size of the SNS) for our experiment.

We observe a significant positive effect (p value < 0.05) of the SNS as plotted in the figure below. We also observed that Copying and Paraphrasing tasks are more positively correlated than the Summarizing task.

6 Conclusion

From the experiments performed on our data, we observed that while there is no significant impact

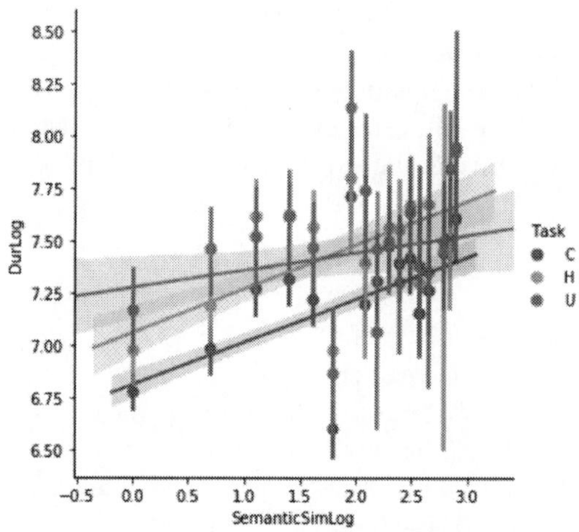

of Orthographic Neighbours, we can see a significant correlation of Semantic Neighbours on the Word Production time. With the high p-value (0.46) for orthographic similarity, we can reject the negative correlation as insignificant and thus conclude that we do not see any impact of Orthographic neighbours on the word production time. For Semantic Similarity, we found positive correlation for all the tasks, with Copying task having least average Dur and Summarizing task having a lesser correlation than the other two tasks. We can therefore conclude, our experiment supports the hypothesis that the activation of larger number of semantically similar words may possibly create more ambiguity in the mind of the user to make a suitable choice which eventually may lead to longer word-production time.

7 Future Enhancements

We would like to expand the scope of our experiment to translation data from multiple languages in the future. We would like to test the theory of 'language non-selective lexical access' that is the co-activation of many word candidates from different languages that are similar to the input word. We would also like to train our own model in multiple languages with Word2Vec for our Bilingual experiments.

References

Carl, Bangalore, Schaeffer. 2016. New Directions in Empirical Translation Process Research

Dana M. Basnight-Brown, Ph.D.: Models of Lexical Access and Bilingualism

Ton Dijkstra, Alexander Wahl. (2018) Multilink: A computational model for Bilingual word recognition and translation

Tomas Mikolov, Kai Chen, Greg Corrado, Jeffrey Dean. (2013) : Efficient Estimation of Word Representations in Vector Space

Ernst-August Gutt (2010), Ph.D, University of London: Translation and Relevance

Predicting Cognitive Effort in Translation Production

Yuxiang Wei
Centre for Translation and Textual Studies
Dublin City University
Ballymun Road, Dublin 9
Dublin, Ireland
yuxiang.wei3@mail.dcu.ie

Abstract

In view of the "predictive turn" in Translation Studies (Schaeffer et al., 2019), there has been increasing interest in investigating particular features of the text which can predict translation efficiency and the cognitive load of translating and post-editing. However, hypotheses of such kinds have often been on the basis of descriptive means in lack of rigorous statistical test on a large scale. In this regard, this paper seeks to empirically study the cognitive effort of translating and Machine Translation (MT) post-editing in relation to different predictor variables including word frequency, word translation entropy, and syntactic choice entropy, making use of a large dataset from the CRITT Translation Process Research Database (CRITT TPR-DB, see Carl et al., 2016) which incorporates multiple languages and translation production modes.

Cognitive effort is measured by eye-movement behavioural data, assuming that an increase in the number or duration of eye fixations on particular words or lexical items of the text indicates an extra processing cost in producing the translation of the corresponding items. These measures of cognitive effort are statistically correlated with frequency and entropy values of the Source Text words, followed by a qualitative analysis of the instances where these variables tend to cause increased processing effort in the translating and post-editing process.

With a particular focus on ambiguity resolution and the influence of formulaic expressions, the qualitative analysis intends to explain whether and how the resolution of the competition between different interpretations of a potentially ambiguous item causes additional processing effort in translating and post-editing, as well as to study the influence of context on this disambiguation process. This analysis complements the statistical correlation between the eye fixation data and the frequency/entropy values of the source text, in an effort to explore dependable means for predicting the cognitive effort of translating and post-editing.

This investigation sheds light on possible correlations of the statistical metrics of the textual material to fixation-based measurements of cognitive effort in translation production, so that the effort can be predicted via these variables. Complemented by the qualitative analyses, it also contributes to the description, explanation, and prediction of translating and post-editing behaviour.

References

Carl, Michael, Moritz Schaeffer, and Srinivas Bangalore. 2016. The CRITT Translation Process Research Database. In Michael Carl, Srinivas Bangalore, and Moritz Schaeffer (Eds.), *New Directions in Empirical Translation Process Research* (pp. 13-54). New York: Springer.

Schaeffer, Moritz, Jean Nitzke, and Silvia Hansen-Schirra. 2019. Predictive turn in translation studies: Review and prospects. In Stanley D. Brunn and Roland Kehrein (Eds.), *Handbook of the Changing World Language Map*. Cham, Switzerland: Springer.

Computerized Note-taking in Consecutive Interpreting: A Pen-voice Integrated Approach towards Omissions, Additions and Reconstructions in Notes

Huolingxiao Kuang
Durham University
Dep.t of Modern Languages and Cultures
England, United Kingdom
huolingxiao.kuang@durham.ac.uk

Abstract

Although note-taking has received extensive attention from scholars in interpreting studies, most of the discussions focus on the descriptive features of notes and derive from personal experience with no empirical support. Instead of solely focusing on the product of note-taking, i.e. notes, where many contradictory findings about note pattern and its connections with interpreting performance were witnessed, this study proposes and practices an innovative approach to visualize the process of note-taking and review the composition of notes. It is expected to find efficient note-taking strategies for interpreters who always find it hard to apply the proposed principles in their own note-taking due to the high individuality of notes.

By replaying the note-taking process recorded by a *Wacom* smart pen and *FlashBack* (an open screen recorder) in *ELAN* (a free annotation toolkit), the researcher can annotate the starting time, the finishing time and the intended meaning of each note, thus coding notes into computerized data (NT standing for note-taking text). After automatic speech transcription (ASR) and manual correction of the source text (ST) and target text (TT), note-taking transcription can be concatenated with ST, and then then imported into CRITT Translation Process Database (CRITT TPR-DB) for alignment.

One distinctive feature of this dataset is its unparalleled nature. During interpreting, interpreters always filter and process the input information by taking advantage of their personal experience, world knowledge and specialized knowledge. It is therefore very common to find additions, omissions and reconstructions in TT and NT. This explains why during ST-TT alignment, renderings with no correspondence in ST are not aligned. This phenomenon is even more prominent in ST-NT alignment (the alignment of the ST with the notes that were taken during the listening phase) since notes are a by-product of ST understanding and a predecessor of TT production, rather than a shorthand of neither the ST nor the TT.

By observing how unparalleled nature develops, interpreters' note-taking preferences, such as grammatical focus (subjects, verbs, etc.), information selection (proper nouns, numbers, etc.), note quantity and note-taking strategies (ellipse, restricting and high condensation), can be identified and further linked with interpreting performance. In addition, ear-pen span - which refers to the time lag between the source text input and the production of notes - can be a valuable indicator of cognitive load, implying the difficulty of language processing at the given interpreting environment.

Computerization, therefore, carves out a new path for note-taking researchers to dig into both the product and process of note-taking. Linking note choices and note-taking behaviours with ST input and TT production provides researchers a precious opportunity to answer the kernel question in note-taking research: how to reduce processing capacity and time requirements of note-taking while maintain the efficiency of notes" (Gile,1995/2009, p. 178).

References

Gile, Daniel (1995, 2009). *Basic Concepts and Models for Interpreter and Translator Training*. Amsterdam: John Benjamins.

Automatization of subprocesses in subtitling

Anke Tardel
Johannes Gutenberg University Mainz and TRA&CO Center Germersheim
antardel@uni-mainz.de

Silvia Hansen-Schirra
Johannes Gutenberg University Mainz and TRA&CO Center Germersheim
hansenss@uni-mainz.de

Silke Gutermuth
Johannes Gutenberg University Mainz and TRA&CO Center Germersheim
gutermsi@uni-mainz.de

Moritz Schaeffer
Johannes Gutenberg University Mainz and TRA&CO Center Germersheim
mschae01@uni-mainz.de

Abstract

There has been noticeable growth in the use of intralingual and interlingual subtitling due to technological advances and accessibility legislation. The process of subtitling, however, has yet to be thoroughly investigated with empirical methods. Given that subtitling is a complex task, interpreting keylogging and eyetracking data in the overall process can be complicated. We therefore focus on the subprocesses involved in subtitling, i.e. transcription and translation of movie dialogue. With advancements in neural machine translation (NMT) especially with creative texts (Toral et al. 2018), research in this special field of translation becomes even more essential to find meaningful ways of improving subtitling processes and informing subtitling training. This development is focus of CompAsS (Computer-Assisted Subtitling), a project funded by the EU and managed by ZDF Digital and University of Mainz with the aim to improve current subtitling processes.

Within CompAsS an exploratory study was carried out where the transcription and translation processes of 13 professional subtitlers and 13 translation students were recorded. Participants performed eight intralingual and interlingual transcription tasks. Here we focus on the results of the three post-editing tasks from Swedish via English (pivot language) into German. Participants post-edited three automatically translated German transcripts of three two-minute video snippets of a Swedish crime series. The Swedish transcripts were first machine translated from Swedish into English and after post-editing further machine translated into German. Participants had to post-edit under three different conditions: a) with access to the Swedish video and the post-edited English transcript, b) only with access to the Swedish video and c) without access to the video and only with the English transcript. For the NMT Google Translate was used. Participants had a translation brief to produce high quality transcripts of the dialogue in the videos; there was no time limit and participants were able to research online.

The tasks were recorded in Translog-II (Carl 2012) with a plugin for eyetracking which allows for a fine-grained analysis of activities such as revisions, and source and target text reading. In combination with screen recording and eyetracking it is possible to observe when and where participants look in the video or text, while producing the transcripts. Triangulating the data with questionnaire ratings, we observe the impact of access to the video and English relay transcript during post-editing of NMT regarding attention distribution, technical and temporal effort. The results in terms of time and quality guide the conception of a new subtitling tool. For the analysis of effort, we use established measures based on gaze and typing data, and subjective ratings (de Sousa, Aziz & Specia, 2011; Vieira, 2016). Our hypotheses were that post-editing is faster than translation tasks from scratch and that access to the video is essential for the post-editing task even if the source language is unknown. The results will be presented with statistical analyses per participant group and condition and combined in linear mixed-effects models.

References

Carl, M., 2012. Translog-II: a Program for Recording User Activity Data for Empirical Translation Process Research. *Proceedings of the LREC 2012. The 8th International Conference on Language Resources and Evaluation*; Istanbul, Turkey: 153–162.

de Sousa, S., Aziz, W. & Specia, L. (2011). 'Assessing the Post-Editing Effort for Automatic and Semi-Automatic Translations of DVD Subtitles', in *Proceedings of the International Conference Recent Advances in Natural Language Processing 2011*, Hissar, Bulgaria: 97–103.

Toral, A., Wieling, M., Way, A., 2018. Post-editing Effort of a Novel With Statistical and Neural Machine Translation. *Frontiers in Digital Humanities* 5. https://doi.org/10.3389/fdigh.2018.00009

Vieira, L. N. (2016). 'How do measures of cognitive effort relate to each other? A multivariate analysis of post-editing process data', Machine Translation, 30(1–2), pp. 41–62.

Correlating Metaphors to Behavioural Data: A CRITT TPR-DB-based Study

Faustino Dardi
Durham University
Dept. of Modern Languages and Cultures
England, United Kingdom
faustino.dardi@durham.ac.uk

Abstract

There exist a strong correlation between the number of translation options available for a certain word and the translator's eye movements. Indeed, higher translation entropy (*HTra*) has been shown to increase uncertainty in translation choices, thus making the translation process costlier, whereas lower entropy facilitates the translation of a particular word into its target rendition.

This exploratory study has been carried out at Kent State University during the second MEMENTO boot camp, and seeks to explore how translation entropy values relate to metaphors and how these correlate to behavioural data. This is achieved by retrieving and analysing existing datasets contained in the CRITT TPR-DB. Datasets with the English-Spanish language pair (BML12, six texts) are analysed in order to explore the correlation between metaphors and behavioural data. Metaphors are annotated in the source text files and then correlated to their renditions in the target texts. The identification of different types of metaphors in the source texts is performed through the application of the updated version of the *Metaphor Identification Procedure* (MIP) developed at Vrije Universiteit Amsterdam (MIPVU).

The behavioural data in the TRP-DB are analysed on the basis of two parameters: (a) first fixation duration (*FFDur*) on the source-text item(s) used metaphorically; (b) total reading time (*Trts*) on the source-text items used metaphorically. Both measures are assessed and correlated to *HTra*, which has been demonstrated to have a significant effect on both *FFDur* and *Trts*: first fixation durations are shorter for source-text items with low translation entropy than for items with a larger number of translation alternatives. Considering that these latter findings confirm the *Literal Translation Hypothesis* – according to which words are first translated literally –, the same procedure can be tentatively applied to metaphor translation, delving into studies not originally performed to investigate metaphorical language translation. A further insight can be given for cross-lingual distortion (*Cross*) between source- and target-text items, in order to explore how the latter correlates to *FFDur* and *Trts* and, in particular, if any significant difference can be detected when compared to *HTra*.

It is possible to establish additional correlations between *FFDur*, *Trts* and the strategies used for translating the metaphors, and in particular if shorter or longer *FFDur* and *Trts* correspond to certain translation strategies. The framework for classifying the target-text translation of source-text metaphors will include five strategies: (1) the translation of a source-text metaphor into an exact equivalent in the target text (M–M); (2) the translation of a source-text metaphor into another metaphorical phrase with the same meaning in the target text (M1–M2); (3) the paraphrase of a source-text metaphor in the target text (M–P); (4) the translation of a source-text non-metaphor into a metaphor in the target text (NM–M); (5) deletion or omission.

References

Jakobsen, Arnt L., and Kristian T. Hvelplund. 2008. "Eye Movement Behaviour across Four Different Types of Reading Task." *Copenhagen Studies in Language*, 36 (1):103–124.

Krennmayr, Tina. 2008. "Using Dictionaries in Linguistic Metaphor Identification." *Selected Papers from the 2006 and 2007 Stockholm Metaphor Festivals*, edited by Nils-Lennart Johannesson and David C. Minugh, 97–115. Acta Universitatis Stockholmiensis, Stockholm.

Schaeffer, Moritz J., Barbara Dragsted, Kristian T. Hvelplund, Laura W. Balling, and Michael Carl. 2015. "Word Translation Entropy: Evidence of Early Target Language Activation during Reading for Translation." In *New Directions in Empirical Translation Process Research: Exploring the CRITT TPRDB*, edited by Michael Carl, Srinivas Bangalore and Moritz J. Schaeffer, 183–210. Springer, Cham.

Schäffner, Christina. 2004. "Metaphor and Translation: Some Implications of a Cognitive Approach." *Journal of Pragmatics,* 36 (7):1253–1269.

Sjørup, Annette C. 2013. *Cognitive Effort in Metaphor Translation.* Copenhagen Business School, Copenhagen.

Exploring Cognitive Effort in Written Translation of Chinese Neologisms: An Eye-tracking and Keylogging Study

Jinjin Chen
Center for Studies of Translation, Interpreting and Cognition, University of Macau, Taipa, Macau SAR, China
chenjj0601@163.com

Defeng Li
Center for Studies of Translation, Interpreting and Cognition, University of Macau, Taipa, Macau SAR, China
defengli@um.edu.mo

Victoria Lei
Center for Studies of Translation, Interpreting and Cognition, University of Macau, Taipa, Macau SAR, China
viclcl@um.edu.mo

Abstract

Neologisms are newly coined lexical units or existing lexical units that acquire a new sense, and they pose great challenges to translators in conducting translation task (Newmark, 1988). This study, taking cognitive effort as a window, is an attempt to find out how the human mind invests its energy in information processing as well as language production during written translation of Chinese neologisms.

Three research questions are formulated in this study: (1) Are translators more cognitively effortful when doing written translation of Chinese neologisms? (2) Does knowledge of context have an effect on the cognitive effort of translators in translating Chinese neologisms? (3) How translators differ in investing cognitive effort in translating Chinese neologisms from different text types?

Three groups of people are invited to the experiment including professional translators, well-trained graduate translation students, and untrained translation students/bilinguals. They are asked to perform three from-scratch written translation tasks from Chinese to English, after which a retrospective interview is conducted to check their knowledge of context and translation strategy in relation to their tasks. A different text type is used for each of these three tasks, while each text consists of 200 words and 7 Chinese neologisms. Participants' translation outputs are recorded by Translog-II and Tobbi 300. Various indicators of cognitive effort including source text gaze measures, target text gaze measures, and target text keystroke measures are analyzed in connection to the subjects' self-assessment using NASA TLX as well as holistic quality assessment by translator trainers.

It is expected that this study will shed light on whether more cognitive effort is allocated in written translation of Chinese neologisms, as well as elucidate the relationship between cognitive effort and knowledge of context. In addition, the study intends to find clues of the relationship among cognitive effort, text type, translation strategy, and translation quality.

References

Newmark, Peter. 1988. *A Textbook of Translation*. New York: Prentice Hall.

Author Index

Association for Computational Linguistics
209 N. Eighth Street
Stroudsburg, Pennsylvania 18360

ISBN 978-1-5108-9248-4

CURRAN ASSOCIATES INC.
proceedings.com